START-UP
Universal Basic Income

**WITH PROGRESS DOLLARS FROM
THE PRODUCTION PARABOLA**

DON
SOARDS

START-UP
Universal Basic Income

With Progress Dollars
From The
Production Parabola

A Revolutionary System
for Implementing
Universal Basic Income

Discover the secret to unlocking financial abundance. With Progress Dollars, you'll learn the groundbreaking approach to generating funds for all American citizens without raising taxes or making social changes.

DON SOARDS

START-UP: Universal Basic Income

Copyright © 2025 Don Soards
First printing edition 2023

ISBN (Paperback): 978-1-965687-64-2
ISBN (eBook): 978-1-965687-65-9

Printed in the United States of America.

AUCTOREM
HOUSE

Auctorem House
276 5th Ave, Ste 704-2591
New York, NY 10001
www.auctoremhouse.com
1.888.332.7718

CONTENTS

INTRODUCTION

We are concerned about too many human workers being replaced by machines. We should be. The harm we face goes far beyond the trauma faced by individuals who have lost their jobs to machines over past centuries. We are moving deeper into a condition of "Who do these corporations think is going to buy their stuff after they lay us all off?". Our economy is getting smaller.

Fortunately, there is a way forward that will help all individuals and our society as a whole. First, we must understand the production parabola and its opportunities.

Implementing Progress Dollars will give us the maximum Universal Basic Income currently. UBI will rise with technological progress. This will be accomplished without significant inflation or raising any citizen's taxes.

SECTION 1

WHAT IS THE PRODUCTION PARABOLA?

My Dad told me that things seldom stay the same. They are either getting better and better or worse and worse. From 1800 to 2000, the American middle-class economy was getting better and better. Since 2000 it has gotten worse and worse. This concept can be described as a parabola with a relatively flat top (1980 to 2020) during the period middle-class buying power was stagnant and our numbers dropping. We are now declining rapidly. There are two choices: getting worse and worse with status quo economic policy or adopt Progress Dollars from the Production Parabola and get better and better. This book explains progress dollar economics and a simple solution that will be the "tide that lifts all boats."

1. **To produce, we need production capacity and one other thing. What is the other item?**

    Answer: We need someone to buy the product. If we don't have enough customers to purchase our entire product, our company will accumulate unsold inventory and may go out of business.

2. **Where do customers get their money?**

> **Answer:** From jobs. Not everyone has a job, but most money comes from jobs either directly or indirectly. When two people get married, bills are more likely to be paid if at least one of them has a job. Even if someone inherited money, that just means that someone back in the past had a good-paying job and made enough to leave some to future generations. Lottery winners get their winnings from a pool funded by people with jobs.

3. **What happens to production when about half of the labor force loses their jobs to machines?**

> **Answer:** Production drops. When too many customers lose their paychecks, product buying reduces. So, corporations are forced to lower production to avoid unsold inventory.

Production requires *demand* and *production capacity*.

If humans don't spend money on a product (lack of *consumer demand*), businesses will quit making it. We get almost all our money by working for it. The amount of buying power (*consumer demand*) is the fraction of the labor force employed. We will use "H" to represent this fraction.

If there is inadequate *production capacity*, then insufficient quantity will exist. Production capacity is work that humans and machines can do. Production capacity has the human component "H" (the same group of people who have jobs) and the machine component "EM" (machine efficiency "E" multiplied by the fraction of machines "M").

> *Production = demand x production capacity*
>
> $$P = H \times (H + EM)$$

Demand and production capacity <u>do not</u> have a "which came first, the chicken or egg" relationship. Instead, production capacity follows demand, just as "form follows function." One example of form follows function is the form of our buildings having roofs (production capacity) to satisfy the function (demand) of keeping the rain off our heads. Production capacity is created by entrepreneurs to optimize their personal profits based on estimates of future demand.

Consumer Perspective: The consumer perspective of Production equals Demand multiplied by Production Capacity can be illustrated by considering your favorite hamburger drive-up restaurant. Let's use $7.00 for the price of a burger. You drive up to the restaurant (production capacity), wait for a loudspeaker employee to ask, "May I help you?", order one burger, drive to the window, pay $7 (demand), receive one burger, and drive off with your hamburger (production). In this case, the production (one hamburger) is equal to the demand of $7 times the production capacity of one burger/$7. This is shown algebraically as:

$$P = D \times PC$$

1 hamburger (Production) = $7 (demand) x burger/$7 (production capacity)

Instead of dollars, we could use the time spent by a wage earner to earn the seven dollars. For example, if you make $14 per hour, you would need to work one-half hour to pay for the burger. Instead of using work hours as a unit to describe the cost of one burger, we could use your work year. The cost of that burger would be a tiny fraction of your work year. If we wanted to find out the cost of all the goods and services you buy during a year, we could add up all the dollar costs of each item, or we could just refer to that cost as one year of your labor (minus savings which get spent in following years anyway).

To assess the annual United States national demand available to buy goods and services, we sum up all the full-time work years worked in one year. The number of full-time work years by the United States employees is equal to the number of full-time employees in the labor force times the percent of those employees who have a job. We can therefore express our annual national demand in <u>labor force units</u> as a percent of the labor force with jobs. We shall use "H" to represent the fraction of humans in our labor force with full-time jobs. Our national demand in annual labor-force units is "H," the fraction of full-time workers with jobs. (Note, part-time employment is converted to full-time equivalent jobs. Ten employees working half-time are converted to five full-time employees when using "H.")

Entrepreneur Perspective: The entrepreneur perspective is that work is either done by humans or machines. In order to maximize profits, the entrepreneur configures his or her new business (production capacity) to produce goods and services as cheaply as possible. The entrepreneur is in a price war with other competitors producing similar products. If other competitors can produce significantly cheaper, customers will buy from the opponents, and the entrepreneur will go broke.

The efficiency of machines can be compared to humans by a factor we shall term "E," which is the ratio of machine output to one human worker. For example, in the year 1800, at the start of the industrial revolution, approximately 70% of Americans were involved in agriculture. With the invention of the farm tractor and other agricultural machinery, about 2% of the United States population is needed to produce our food in the 21st century. The machine ratio "E" 70%/2% = 35 for the agricultural sector of our economy. During the past two centuries, many farm/ranch workers have left the agricultural sector to enter the manufacturing and service sectors.

I have used an "E" value of 20. On page 34, I reference a sensitivity analysis" that demonstrates that E values of 10, 20, 50, and 100 give very similar results and suggest the same course of action needed for our economic well-being.

Since machines are so much more productive than human workers, the entrepreneur is forced to replace human workers with machines whenever possible, just to keep up with competing businesses. As machines get better and cheaper, the pressure to automate human worker jobs becomes more intense. Employing humans requires paying overtime, annual leave, sick leave, maternity leave, holiday wages, employer contributions to social security, raises in the minimum wage, general wage increases due to inflation, break times, 401K matching contributions, and retirement plan matching contributions. Other entrepreneur expenses include employee parking, impacts on workflow when employees can't attend work due to inclement weather, being sick, having personal business to attend to, having a death in the family, etc. Employee complaints can also be emotionally taxing. Employee theft is a major problem in many businesses. Robots and other machines do not have these costly and distracting problems.

We will use the term "M" to represent the fraction of human work taken over by machines (expressed in the same units as H). The equation for production capacity can now be expressed as the sum of work done by people (H) plus the work done by machines (EM). Production capacity = H + EM

The equation:

Production = Demand X Production Capacity now becomes **P = H x (H+EM)**.

A table for a machine efficiency of E = 20 (this is for machines that produce a rate of 20 human workers) follows.

The most important concept to notice in this table is that total national production rises as employment goes from 100% to slightly above 50%, then starts dropping when employment goes below that level. Other useful concepts are that the rising section is labeled "seller's market" (too many dollars chasing too few goods), and the falling sector is labeled "buyer's market" (too few dollars chasing too many goods). The buyer's market dilemma was explained to me by a student I was privileged to tutor as "Who do these corporations think is going to buy their stuff after they lay us all off?"

To help understand the equation in table format, here are two examples. We start off with all humans (100%) and no machines (0%). This would be at the start of the industrial revolution in 1800. The term "H" for humans in decimal format is "1.0," and the term "M" for machines is "0.0". Production "P" equals demand H (the fraction of humans with a job back then) H times the production capacity of 1.0 (all work being done by humans) plus 0.0 for having no heavy equipment. Production P = 1 x 1 = 1 National Labor Force Year of Production.

If we go to the second line in the table, we have the condition where the machines have advanced to do 10% of the work and humans do 90%. The production becomes $P = H \times (H + EM) = 0.9 \times (0.9 + 20 \times 0.1) = 0.9 \times (0.9 + 2.0) = 0.9 \times 2.9 = 2.61$ National Labor Force Years of Production. Having machines do a small fraction of our work increased our national output to 261%!

$$P = H \times (H+EM)$$

For a machine efficiency of 20 x human labor, we get the following table:

Humans Working (percent)	Machines (percent)	Demand "H"	Production Capacity "H+EM"	Production P = H(H+EM) E = 20	
100	0	**1.0**	1.0	1.0	Seller's Market
90	10	**0.9**	2.9	2.61	Seller's Market
80	20	**0.8**	4.8	3.84	Seller's Market
70	30	**0.7**	6.7	4.69	Seller's Market
60	40	0.6	8.6	5.16	Seller's Market
50.63	49.37	0.5063	10.3803	5.2555	Maximum Production
50	50	0.5	10.5	5.25	Buyer's Market
40	60	0.4	**12.4**	4.96	Buyer's Market
30	70	0.3	**14.3**	4.29	Buyer's Market
20	80	0.2	**16.2**	3.24	Buyer's Market
10	90	0.1	**18.1**	1.81	Buyer's Market
0	100	0	**20**	0	Buyer's Market

Bold numbers are high demand and high production capacity.

Italicized numbers are low demand and low production capacity.

In our high employment (high demand periods), technology improves the production capacity, and the multiple of high demand and advancing technology enhances our standard of living (higher production). After reaching peak production, technology keeps improving our production capacity, but the multiple of stronger technology multiplied by weaker demand (lower employment) gives us lower production and a lower standard of living. Oops!

Here is a graph of the Production Parabola and machine efficiency of 20 times human labor $P = H \times (H + 20 \times M)$

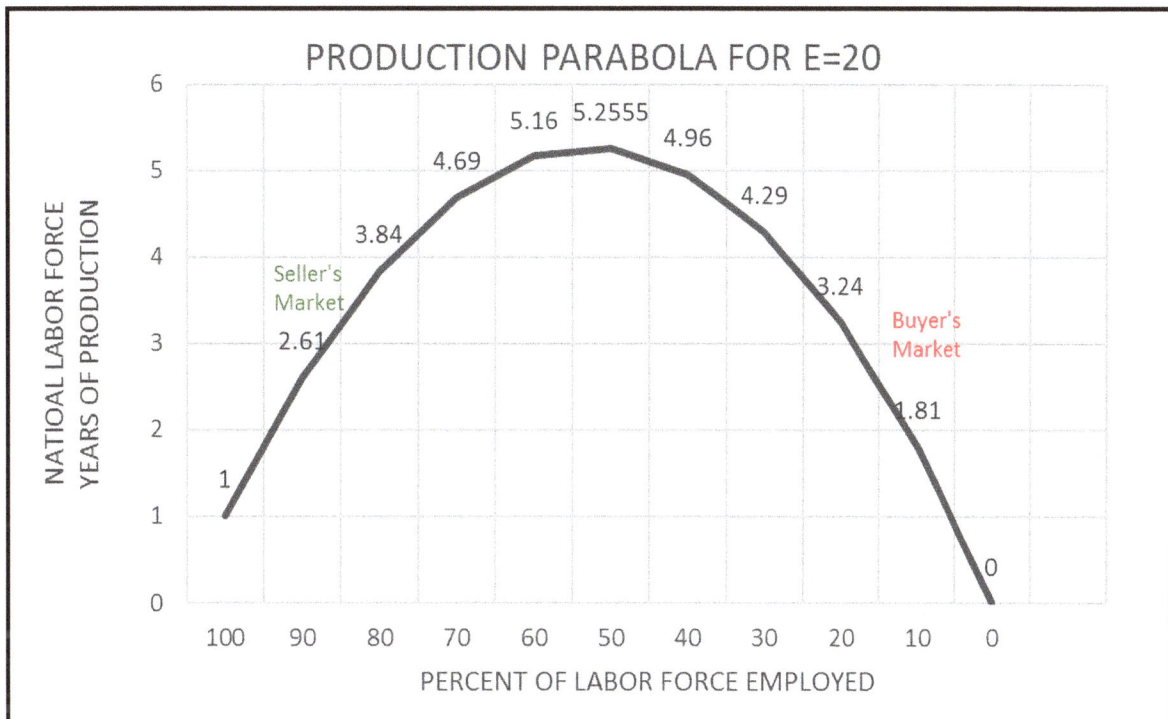

PRODUCTION PARABOLA FOR E=20

The seller's market side of the production parabola has high demand and low production capacity.

The buyer's market side shows technology increasing production capacity but lowering demand so much that consumers can't purchase all we could make. Production has to be cut back to avoid unsold merchandise. Production cuts usually mean laying off workers, which further lowers consumer demand.

ADVANTAGE OF LIVING IN A BUYER'S MARKET USING PROGRESS DOLLARS TO MAKE UP WAGES LOST TO AUTOMATION

Entering the buyer's market is good because we can now **distribute Progress Dollar UBI to every adult US citizen from a non-taxpayer pot of money (Progress Dollars) to increase demand enough to make up for wages lost to automation.** As our technology grows, the Progress Dollar UBI grows over time.

WHICH SIDE OF THE PRODUCTION PARABOLA ARE WE ON?

Economies are very complex. There is no single mathematical equation that defines all the economic behavior of a nation's citizens. Here are eleven facts that indicate we have moved from a seller's market to a buyer's market as we entered the 21st century.

1. Percent of the total labor force employed full-time is near or below the peak of the production parabola.

Civilian Labor Force Participation

Bureau of Labor Statistics

Looking back at the Production Parabola table from the previous section, we see that the production peaks at a full-time employment of slightly greater than 50%. So where are we now? The October 2017 labor participation rate of 62.7% included unemployed people who had looked for work during the previous weeks. Without those unemployed, the labor-force participation rate fell to 60.2%. This number reduces to 53.7% when part-time work is converted to full-time (see page 34). When artificial job-creating factors like federal deficit spending and lowering of interest rates are considered, we are likely in a buyer's market employment condition. (Note, I am using pre-Covid pandemic data because I feel it is more representative of our overall economic condition since 2000. I will address the pandemic cost-push inflation and raised interest rates in a later section.)

2. Since we are losing jobs, we start spending money at a slower rate. After 2000, the velocity of money spent dropped sharply.

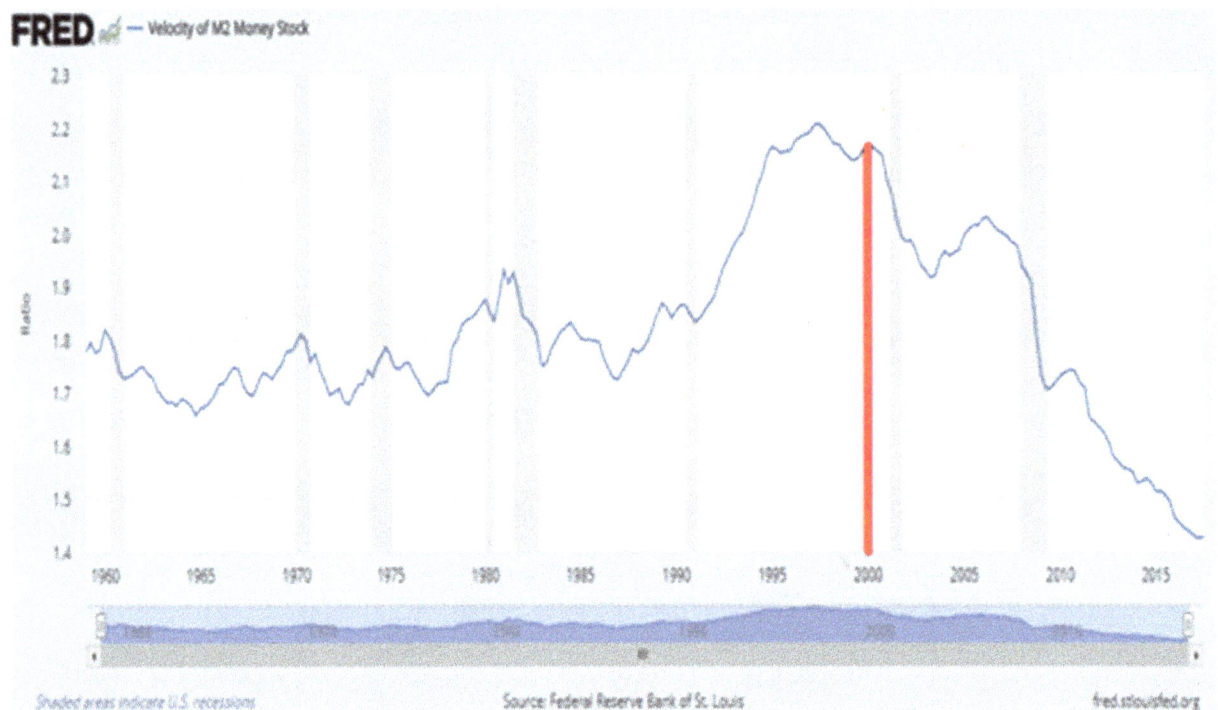

The velocity of money declined from being spent 2.1 times per year in 2000 to about 1.4 times per year by 2017. Those who still have a job are scared and cut back spending.

3. As people spend less, our gross domestic product (national output of goods and services) declines. The decline started in 2006. We are slipping deeper down the buyer's market side of the production parabola.

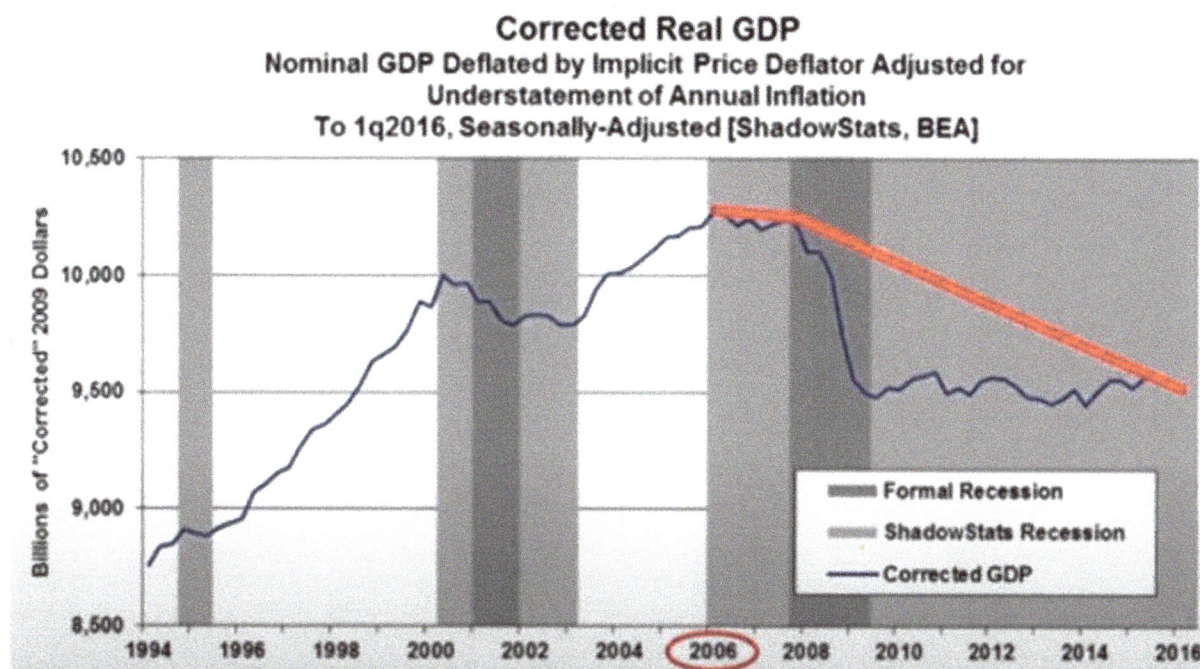

Corrected Real GDP
Nominal GDP Deflated by Implicit Price Deflator Adjusted for Understatement of Annual Inflation
To 1q2016, Seasonally-Adjusted [ShadowStats, BEA]

4. The official unemployment rate radially understates real unemployment. This is good for electing incumbent politicians but bad for informing voters to take action on a huge economic vulnerability. The economy is not OK.

After I discovered the production parabola in the spring of 2016, I spent several months discovering how useful the buyer's market concept was at explaining many elements in our current economy. Once I realized that we could and should give progress dollars (from a non-taxpayer pot of money) to every adult citizen to replenish the wages lost to automation, I began talking to others and posting white papers on the internet. I sent the white papers out to economics professors for review. I became confident enough to approach a political official. I talked to a staffer, and he said there was no problem because the unemployment rate was so low (about 4% at that time)!

So, how did we go from 22% unemployed to 4%? The reason is that the official statistic does not include those unemployed workers who have been discouraged for more than a year. Fortunately, ShadowStats.com has computed a graph that includes such unemployed workers.

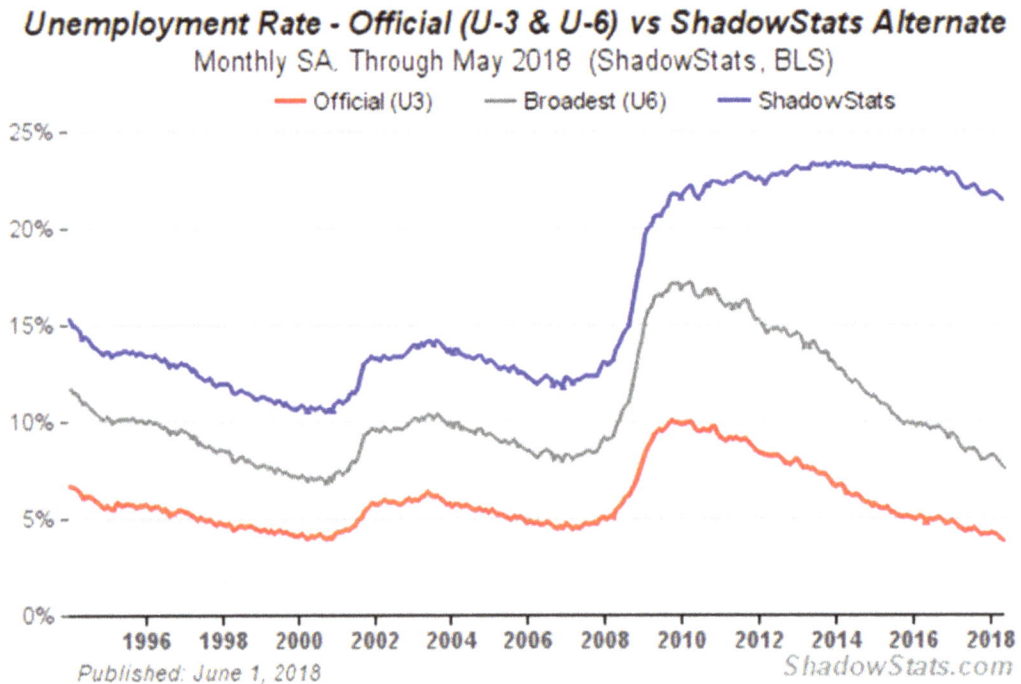

Unemployment Rate - Official (U-3 & U-6) vs ShadowStats Alternate
Monthly SA. Through May 2018 (ShadowStats, BLS)

— Official (U3)　　— Broadest (U6)　　— ShadowStats

Published: June 1, 2018　　ShadowStats.com

The bottom two lines are the Bureau of Labor Statics U3 and U6 values, and the top line includes the rest of the discouraged workers. Since 2010, the U6 one-year-or-less discouraged worker graph dropped from about 17% to about 8%, while the comprehensive-discouraged-unemployed worker (ShadowStats graph) has remained in the 22% range.

This means about 9% of the workforce has gone from short-term to long-term discouraged during the last eight years!

The buyer's market side of the production parabola simply does not require as much human labor as the previous seller's market because machines are getting more sophisticated and cheaper.

The notion that unemployment is low is fake news. This fake news is released to the public to benefit incumbent officeholders and get them re-elected. Our real rate of unemployment is well above 20%. Fortunately, our society has safety nets like free food distribution, so people don't starve.

The unemployment graph shows the government's U3 (official rate) and U6 dropping rapidly. <u>This is because more and more people put out of work by automation have been out of work for over a year and got dropped out of the official unemployment statistic.</u> If this trend continues, the official rate could drop to zero because everyone who lost their job couldn't get another job for over a year. The idea of having a 0% official unemployment rate if everyone went from desperate to destitute in over a year's time of unemployment, shows the insanity of how misleading the official unemployment rate is. *Do not allow yourself to be bullied by anyone quoting the official unemployment rate. The economy is not OK.*

A real unemployment rate that is so high (22%) is another indicator that we are in a buyer's market. We simply don't need as many workers.

5. Technology creates few jobs.

The purpose of looking at unemployment statistics is not just to show that our unemployment is of similar magnitude to the Great Depression (25%) but to show that we have once again crossed over into the buyer's market. Only this time, the crossover is much worse.

During the Depression, workers dumped off the farm had some chance of leaving the agricultural sector and moving into the manufacturing sector or services sector. Now there is nowhere to go. Automation eliminates most new jobs. Here is a graph of job creation. It shows that from the start of the industrial age (1800) up to 1950, job creation was high during the period when people made machines. By 2000 machines were making machines, and job creation was very slow. (Data for this graph are found on pages 23 to 30 in "Progress Dollars from the Production Parabola" by Don Soards.)

JOB CREATION BY TECHNOLOGY

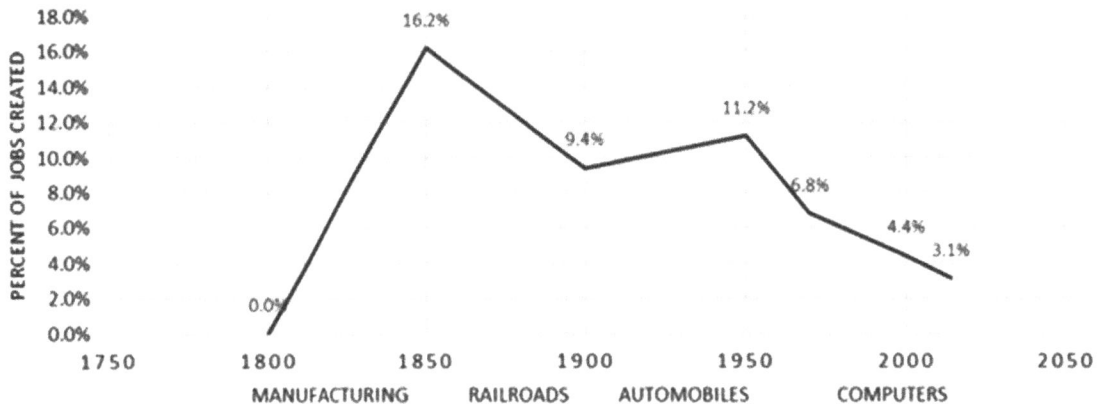

No wonder young people, who have grown up during the computer and information age, believe that automation destroys more jobs than it creates. The data shows that automation hasn't been creating many jobs lately. We have staggeringly high real unemployment and strong prospects for even higher unemployment when artificial intelligence replaces so many more of us.

We have long accepted that manual labor and low-skilled jobs were at risk of being automated. Now, inventions like ChatGPT, which can write computer code, write essays, pass a medical test, create art, etc., in response to verbal commands, demonstrate that even highly skilled knowledge jobs are at risk of being automated.

Can't we just continue to inflate the economy forever and ever? Probably not. Eventually, the debt we are servicing will consume so much money that there will not be enough for the things we need to run this nation. I firmly believe that we need to cut back our spending of taxpayer money from both the rich pot and the bottom 90% pot. Since we are in a buyer's market, we need to avoid making cuts that would reduce consumer spending (i.e., don't cut social programs).

More than ever, we need to augment our economy's consumers with Progress Dollar UBI (from a non-taxpayer pot of money) just to sustain our production capacity. Without a Progress Dollar UBI, our production capacity will decline, and most Americans will not realize the American Dream.

6.   We have record-low marriage rates.

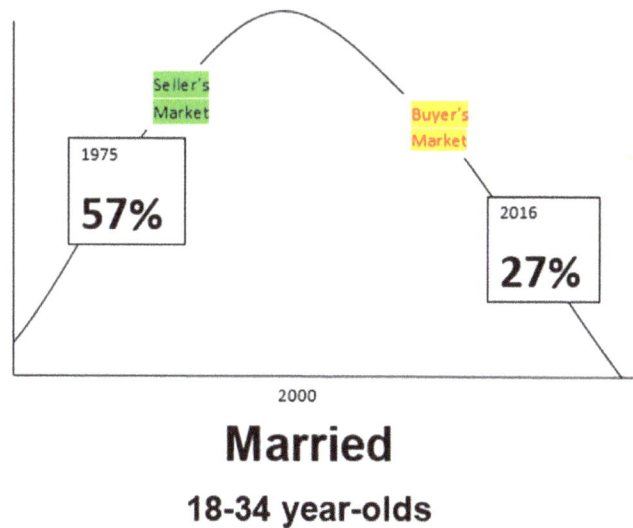

Married

18-34 year-olds

A 2013 Gallup poll shows that 91% of 18–34-year-olds still plan to get married someday. Where their actions place them on the production parabola is stunning. The Great Depression previously had the lowest marriage rate in history because of a lack of income.

Marriage rates are now below those of the Great Depression! Most 18–34-year-olds can't afford to get married. This shows one effect of collapsing income in our buyer's market.

As we go farther down the buyer's market slope, we produce less and need even fewer employees. This disproportionately hits those looking for that first good job that provides enough money to support a family. Some people are concerned that birthrates have fallen below the replacement value of 2.1 children per woman in the industrialized world. The younger generation understands they face declining job prospects in an increasingly automated job market. The future looks bright for the rich who own the machines but not for the rest of us who have only our labor to sell. The American dream is imploding.

7. We experience very low interest rates.

   In a seller's market, we still have unsatisfied demand. It pays to develop new businesses to satisfy new customers. The competition for business loans bids up the cost of money, and interest rates rise. In a buyer's market, we have an over-abundance of production. There are not enough customers to buy all the merchandise produced. Interest rates are low because no one wants to loan to prospective businesses that don't have enough customers.

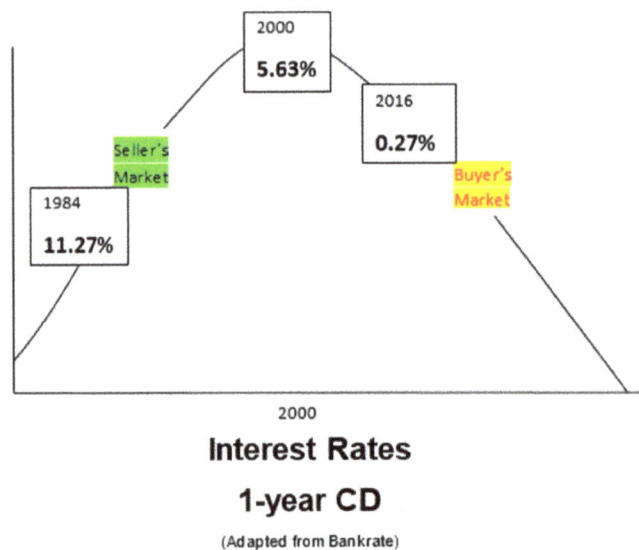

Interest Rates

1-year CD

(Adapted from Bankrate)

8. We are experiencing low asset appreciation.

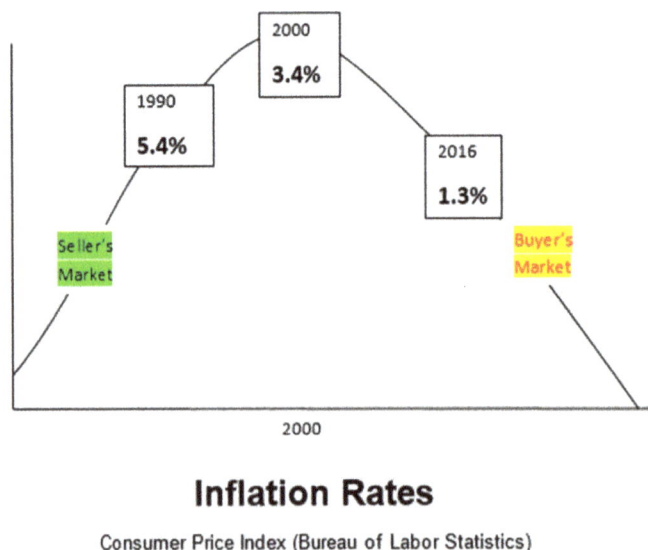

Inflation Rates

Consumer Price Index (Bureau of Labor Statistics)

A seller's market is one with more buyers than merchandise available. A seller's market demand-pull inflation is too many dollars chasing too few goods. We experienced many episodes of demand-pull inflation on the seller's market side of the production parabola.

In our buyer's market, we have little inflation. We have dropped below the Federal Reserve goal of 2% inflation (before the 2020 covid pandemic).

A buyer's market has more merchandise for sale than buyers can purchase. We are getting closer to deflation—too few dollars chasing too many goods.

Understanding that we are in a buyer's market explains why the traditional seller's market "teeter-totter" relationship between inflation and interest rates is broken. In a seller's market, when interest rates were high, demand-pull inflation was low (demand-pull inflation is too many dollars chasing too few goods). The converse of low-interest rates and high demand-pull inflation was also observed during the past century (a seller's market). By 2016 we had both record-low interest rates and meager inflation. We had low inflation because demand is low when automation replaces jobs (wages). We had record low-interest rates because there was little need for new business when fewer people had enough money (good jobs) to sell to.

Employees who work for a business face a double whammy. Their jobs may be automated at their place of employment, or the firm they work for may be out-competed by a more automated competitor (like malls being replaced by internet retailers).

The inflation we experienced during the 2020–2022 period was cost-push inflation due to the covid pandemic, war in Ukraine, bird flu, climate irregularities, etc. The solution to cost-push inflation is patience, Progress dollar UBI, and capitalism.

9. Jobs are harder to find.

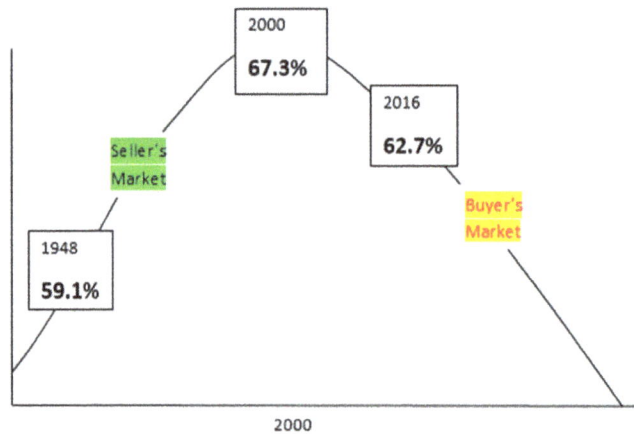

2000
67.3%

2016
62.7%

Seller's Market

Buyer's Market

1948
59.1%

2000

Labor Force Participation Rate

(Bureau of Labor Statistics)

The percentage of the US population with jobs has been declining since we entered the buyer's market in 2000.

Think you are going to work forever? Maybe you will, but doing what job? One of my fellow tutors explained to me that age 53 was a cutoff for hiring. At that age, you are considered to be too expensive, have skills that are out-of-date, or both. My experience meeting former workers of a world-famous manufacturer where I live is consistent with the age 53 cutoff. These individuals were treated disrespectfully and finally quit or were "laid off."

10. Do no better than my parents did.

Each generation hopes that the next generation will do better than it did. Parents hope that things are better for their children than what the parents experienced in their own lives. This graph shows that those born in 1940 had a 90% chance of making more than their parents did at age 30. That percentage has dropped to only 50% for those born in 1984. This trend is alarming. At the 50% rate, the economic quality of life is no longer increasing for the next generation. This would be expected as one crosses the top of the production parabola and begins a downhill slide into the buyer's market.

Absolute mobility has plummeted

Percentage of children earning more than their parents, by birth cohort

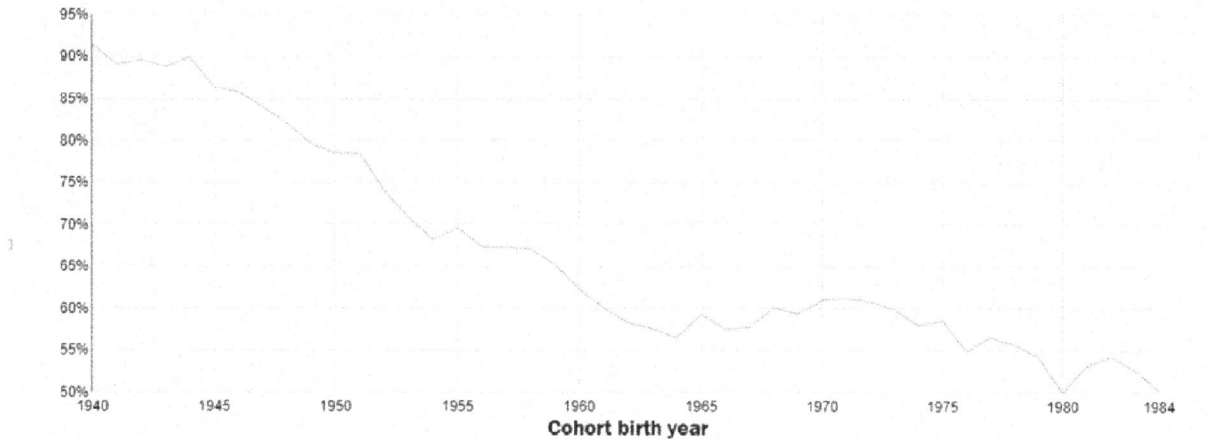

Cohort birth year

Source: Chetty et al. "The Fading American Dream: Trends in Absolute Income Mobility Since 1940." Science 356(6336): 398-406, 2017. Figure 1B. Data downloaded from www.equality-of-opportunity.org/data/

BROOKINGS

There is an old joke about an automated manufacturing plant staffed by a human and a dog.

The human is responsible for seeing that the plant is running smoothly, and the dog's job is to make sure the human doesn't touch anything.

As machinery gets more advanced, the need for human workers declines. As the number of paychecks (and their amounts) decline, production is reduced to avoid excess inventory. Our national production per citizen declines, our standard of living drops, and for more and more of us, the American dream vanishes.

11.   Problems everywhere.

Seller's-market side	Buyer's-market side
Increasing middle class	Declining middle class
America is a great nation.	"Make America great again."
Education is a good investment.	Massive student debt without jobs

Invest in production to profit.	Demand is decreasing—Cash is King.
Businesses grow sales.	Companies cut costs.
Full-time jobs	Part-time jobs, discouraged workers
Good job benefits	Declining benefits
Funded retirements	401Ks
Hiring	Layoffs
Want cable TV	Millions "Cut the Cord."
Large to moderate inflation	Deflation or meager inflation
Individual families having their own home	Multi-generational families in one home
Rising salaries	Jobless recovery
High velocity of money (It gets spent often)	Low velocity of money
Low credit card debt	High credit card debt
Hope	Fear for the future

The preceding indications point to the American economy leaving the seller's market and entering the buyer's market side of the production parabola. We have gone from "build a better mouse trap, and the world will beat a path to your door" (production capacity is weak) to "who do these corporations think are going to buy their stuff after they lay us all off" (demand is weak).

Fortunately, being in a buyer's market gives us a new, wonderful opportunity.

WHAT IS OUR OPPORTUNITY?

One pressing question will become, "Can we continue to inflate as we move deeper into the buyer's market side of the production parabola?" After World War II, we had more dollars than goods, so paying interest was relatively easy. Around 2000, we were at the flat top of the production parabola and still had considerable purchasing power. Now we have started sliding into the "too few dollars" part of the curve. Continuing to borrow introduces too many vulnerabilities into our national economy. For example, increases in interest rates may shock our economy, and large increases might even topple our government. We need to abandon the old two-pot model of wages and taxes.

Fortunately, we have a third pot of money–progress dollars. Progress dollars are the financial weapon of choice to optimize production during a buyer's market because they directly target low consumer demand. The problem with old weapons like tax cuts is that they target old seller's market challenges by getting money into the hands of the rich so they can make more production capacity. Our problem is low demand, not low productivity.

The great historian Arnold Toynbee said, "Nothing fails like success." His observation of the fall of great societies was that they continued to use the tools that made them successful against old challenges causing them to cope poorly with new challenges. President Franklin Roosevelt used the two-pot tool of Keynesian economics, which utilizes taxpayer money for stimulus during the "bust years" and then replaces that money during the "boom years." Eventually, he called a halt to using taxpayer money for fear that it would be difficult to pay it back. Keynesian economics was a tool created during the seller's market that was too weak to continue consumer income augmentation once we slipped into the Great Depression buyer's market.

Progress dollars are the third pot of money. Progress dollars are never repaid. They are an economic stimulus that functions as a *de facto* income augmentation. We have been attempting economic stimulus with ill-targeting overspending for far too long.

What will happen when we use the Progress Dollar UBI? The lower 90% will immediately benefit. They will use that money to feed, shelter, and entertain their families. The rich are better at competing for money in that economic poker game we know as our competitive capitalism. Money will slowly migrate from the lower 90% pot to the rich pot, where it can be employed to create more production capacity. At the top of the production parabola, we will generate the most tax revenue, and that can be used to pay back our debts.

Three-pot capitalism will give our culture unprecedented prosperity. Our current two-pot (wages and taxes) capitalism is taking us deeper down the buyer's market side of the production parabola.

If voters panic and elect leaders who institute two-pot socialism, our decline will be faster. The problem with socialism is that it is only about half as productive as capitalism. Going to socialism will give individuals an equal share of a much small pie. Stay away from socialism.

The worst thing we can do in our current buyer's market is a Hoover-like strategy of reducing consumer spending with tax increases or government spending cuts without using the progress-dollar pot to support the economy. Let's pay our debts while keeping our economy strong. We now have the understanding to do both with the progress-dollar third pot.

The stimulus money needs to be printed, not borrowed. The stimulus money is not appropriated funds. Stimulus money is taken from a "free and clear" account without any obligation to pay it back in the future. Our current money is backed by the full faith and credit of the United States government. Stimulus money is backed by the full faith and credit of the United States government with an economy producing maximum output.

During the past seller's market, we didn't dare increase the money supply for fear of creating massive inflation. However, in our current buyer's market, we have too few buyers with adequate cash. We need to supplement our buyers with brand-new printed money without any obligation of taking it back from future generations who are most likely to be in a buyer's market themselves.

Changing the law to allow the US government to print money (off the balance sheet) and distribute it to US adult consumers will give us the prosperity on which to base our future society while allowing the rich to keep their capital.

The stimulus is not socialism. Socialism is the central planning of resources and social ownership of critical assets. Capitalism is individual planning of resources and personal ownership of assets. Giving money to individuals who make their own decisions about which assets to purchase is capitalism. Note that capitalism does not qualify how individuals get money. They might have gotten wages from a job, inherited it, collected social security, received a tax break, or received monthly UBI checks.

The stimulus is not a "free lunch." Effort by someone is required to create wealth. The question of "how can printed money be of benefit if no one earned it?" can be answered by the fact that generations of innovators earned it through their creation of ever more advanced technology. That technology has brought us to the place of too little money and too much extra production, and now it is time to make "too little" into "just right" by issuing monthly UBI checks.

Won't wealth trickle down from the rich to the middle class? No. The evidence says that the rich get richer and the poor get poorer. The bottom 90% has seen its share of income drop from 68% down to 53% during the past 35 years (from "Percents of Incomes" from MarketWatch September 12, 2016, article using data from HowMuch.net).

Isn't the economy too complicated to forecast accurately? Respecting complexity doesn't mean we should be afraid of it. The procedure for complex situations is to go slow. Navigating complex situations is like driving in a fog with limited visibility; you drive slow enough to have adequate time to react to obstacles in your path.

I suggest we respect economic complexity by increasing monthly stimulus check amounts in $100 increments until we see some signs of seller's market (demand-pull) inflation. Since almost everyone has a social security number, I recommend that the Social Security Administration distribute the UBI money using social security numbers to reference each adult American citizen. The authority to order UBI increases should be given to the Federal Reserve. I recommend a limit of $1000 per month in the initial legislation.

PROGRESS DOLLARS

UBI "Progress dollars" are economic stimulus money paid to every American citizen over the age of eighteen to replace human wages lost to automation.

One of the biggest fears people have when first hearing about "printed money" is inflation and the 20th-century belief that their money will be worthless. Inflation is "too much money chasing too few goods." Before the year 2000, printing money caused seller's-market currency to inflate.

Such is not the case in our 21st-century buyer's-market economy. We now have too few dollars chasing too many goods. This book makes a case for augmenting the "too few" to become the "just right" amount of spending money to boost our productivity to the top of the production parabola, where our money is worth more because we have a maximum number of goods and services available to buy. This optimum purchasing power and the progress dollar UBI we receive should alleviate inflation fears.

What has not been covered thus far is the realization that the production parabola is constantly growing. The value of "E," the efficiency ratio of machine work to human labor, is continually increasing. In other words, we are making more goods than we have in the past. Merely replacing wages previously lost to existing automation is not enough to minimize layoffs. We must also increase progress-dollar funding to buy the additional amount of goods created by improving technology. Otherwise, companies will be in a position of having production capacity in excess of consumer demand. This will cause companies to lower productive capacity by laying off employees rather than accumulating unsold inventory. To avoid sliding back down the buyer's-market deflationary curve, we need to create progress dollars that replace the paychecks lost to existing automation and give us the additional purchasing power to buy the new goods created by technological progress. Progress dollar monthly stimulus checks should increase about $25 every year

The basic strategy is to have the Federal Reserve direct the Social Security Administration to send ever-increasing amounts of progress dollars in the form of UBI checks to adult citizens until a small amount of seller's-market inflation is observed. Once seller's-market (demand-pull) inflation is observed, authorities should stop raising the UBI amounts. After this pause, the UBI should be raised in small increments.

Note that a small amount of low-demand buyer's-market inflation in the 1 to 2% range may continue throughout this period. This condition happens when demand declines, pushing up unit costs.

ADVANTAGES OF $500 PER MONTH UBI

Eventually, we will reach a monthly stimulus amount of $500 per American citizen over the age of 18. Getting $500 per month accumulates to $6,000 per year. Here are some of the advantages.

School loans paid off: The average school loan is in the $24,000 to $30,000 range. Many students take 4 to 5 years to complete college. During that time, they would have accumulated $24,000 to $30,000 and can graduate debt free.

Join the middle class: A minimum-wage job makes approximately $14,000 per year. If you add the stimulus to that, you get $20,000 per year. If your partner has a minimum-wage job, your family is getting $40,000 per year. Welcome to the American middle class!

Afford to retire: Social Security alone is not enough to pay retirement bills. Most people's savings and 401Ks won't make up the difference. Adding $500 per month will. As time goes by, that $500 per month will increase.

Reduce government debt: Robots don't pay taxes. People do. Federal and state governments will benefit directly from taxing the stimulus as income. Additionally, people will have more money to spend. This will increase sales tax revenue to state and local governments. Corporations will create more high-paying jobs as they increase staff to increase production, and that will increase state income tax and federal income tax revenues. Lastly, Social Security will receive more contributions to enable it to last longer.

GETTING $500 PER MONTH EXTRA WILL HELP:

Buy a car
Rent an apartment
Afford to get married
Buy a House

The first $500 is an estimate of what it will take to get back up to the top of the production parabola. The stimulus will increase until we observe a little inflation. After that, UBI monthly raises will grow approximately $25 every year. If artificial intelligence improves productivity at a faster rate, then the stimulus amounts will increase.

Reduce crime: Currently, a car thief leaves prison after five years with little money and has little choice but to steal cars again. However, if this same individual had accumulated $30,000 while in prison and started getting $500 per month, he or she could buy a new car. There would be less incentive to return to a life of crime to survive economically. There would be a great incentive to combine any low-paying job with the UBI and try to survive in our economy rather than return to prison.

Fewer "economic abortions": Some individuals decide to have an abortion based on a lack of income. They can't afford to care for a child and don't want the pain of having it and then giving it away. The higher the UBI, the greater the financial ability to keep the child.

Slash Poverty: An immediate reduction in poverty occurs with the receipt of cash. Additionally, every year allows adult citizens of the United States to receive a UBI increase of approximately $25 per month. After forty years, this amounts to $1000 per month. This, combined with the estimated $500 that we should quickly receive, provides a total of $1,500 per month or $18,000 per year (in 2017 dollars) to every United States adult citizen. The $18,000 per year lifts all adult citizens well above the 2017 federal poverty level of $13,860. Note that the annual UBI increase automatically adjusts upward for deflation.

Shorter workweek: Working a 5-day, 40-hour workweek may no longer be socially desirable. Human workers are being replaced by "automation workers." At some point, we will need a shorter workweek to spread the work across our entire labor pool. We are getting closer to a similar situation faced by President Franklin Roosevelt in the Great Depression when he preferred to have three workers working 40 hours per week rather than two workers working 60 hours per week. Finally...

Hope: The automation stipend given in the form of a monthly UBI check will generate hope that our government cares and has the power to do the right thing. We can now cheer automation rather than fear it.

WE HAVE A CHOICE TO MAKE

Should we stay with outdated sellers' market strategies or take advantage of the buyer's market opportunity to print a moderate amount of money without inflation?

No Action Required	UBI Checks
School loan debt	Paid-off school loans
Declining middle class	Increasing middle class
Work full-time until you are out of time.	Afford to retire or work by choice
More government debt	Reduced government debt
Declining health care	Additional money to spend on health
Longer workweek	Shorter workweek
More crime	Less crime
Rising poverty	Slash poverty

If you understand that we are on the buyer's market side of the production parabola, please contact the elected federal officials representing you. Ask them for legislation to allow Progress Dollar UBI payments for adult United States citizens.

Automation can continue to benefit American society if we adopt the Progress Dollar UBI. Previously, I estimated that we needed about $500 per adult citizen per month. While that estimate may be high, it may also be low. I recommend that the proposed legislation allows for up to $1000 of economic stimulus to provide a range of stimulus responses as needed.

The second factor making things worse that is not included in the production parabola is wage suppression by newer, cheaper technology. At the macro level, we note that the bottom 90% has seen its share of income drop from 68% down to 53% during the past 35 years (from "Percents of Incomes" from MarketWatch Sep 12, 2016, article using data from HowMuch. net). Some of this drop is due to human employees' lack of competitive pricing power relative to increasingly cheaper technological alternatives. Wage suppression translates into lower consumer demand, which drives our economy deeper down the buyer's market side of the production parabola. This is another reason for a more liberal upper limit on economic stimulus legislation.

Note, an extensive Frequently Asked Questions section about Progress Dollars is available on pages 32 to 40 of "Progress Dollars from the Production Parabola" by Don Soards. The same work also contains information on machine coefficient "E", additional production parabola equations, international application, ethics comparisons, etc.

SECTION 4

LEGISLATION

The US government can implement Progress Dollar UBI by amending the Social Security Act.

(Original Signature of Member)

119TH CONGRESS

H.R. __

To optimize national production by replacing consumer demand lost to automation.

_____

IN THE HOUSE OF REPRESENTATIVES

Date: _____

_____ of _____ introduced the following bill; which was referred to the Committee on Ways and Means, Committee on Appropriations, and the Joint Economic Committee.

_____

A BILL

To optimize national production by replacing consumer demand lost to automation.

1   *Be it enacted by the Senate and House of Representatives of the*

2   *United States of America in Congress assembled.*

3   **SECTION 1. SHORT TITLE.**

4   This Act may be cited as the "Progress Dollar UBI Act of 2025."

SEC. 2. PURPOSE.

1   Customers are required to fund production. Advancements in

2   technology have replaced workers with machines and threaten to

3   replace many more in the future. The worker paychecks lost to

4   automation have reduced consumer demand below the optimum

5   required to maximize our gross domestic product. The purpose of

6   this act is to replace consumer demand lost to automation with an

7   amount that minimizes inflation while optimizing our national

8   production of goods and services.

9   **SEC. 3. ECONOMIC STIMULUS DISTRIBUTION**

10 The Social Security Act of 1935 is amended to add—

11 **"TITLE XII ECONOMIC OPTIMIZATION PROGRAM**

12 The Federal Reserve of the United States is

13 hereby authorized to direct the Social Security Administration to

14 distribute up to $1000 per month of Progress Dollar UBI to adult (age

15 eighteen or over) United States citizens. UBI Progress Dollars are not

16 borrowed from the US Treasury. UBI Progress Dollars are not

17 appropriated funds. UBI Progress Dollars are taken from an account

18 that does not permit repayment. UBI Progress Dollars are backed by

19 the full faith and credit of the United States government, with its

20 economy producing at maximum output. UBI Progress Dollars are the

21 amounts of money to be transferred to American citizens over the

22 age of eighteen to replenish the consumer demand lost

23 when machines replace excessive numbers of American workers.

24 UBI Progress Dollars are to be added into the American economy in an

25 amount that optimizes our national production of goods and

26 services.

27 **SEC. 4. EFFECTIVE DATE**

28 The amendment made by this Act shall take effect 90 days

29 after the enactment of this Act.

THREE IMPORTANT POINTS

We can only avoid inflation by adding money during the buyer's market portion of the production parabola when we have "too few dollars chasing too many goods." Once we reach the top of the production parabola, we can no longer add money. If we go back into the seller's market where there are "too many dollars chasing too few goods" and add more money, we will cause hyper-inflation.

When the Federal Reserve puts enough money into our economy to cause slight, temporary inflation, our citizens will easily cope because they receive so much more from UBI. Having adult American citizens receive the progress dollars personally is a much kinder system than having our federal government overspend us into inflation that burdens citizens trying to make ends meet without a monthly progress dollar check. (Note that while large federal projects employ some people, the bulk of the money goes to the contractor who owns the machines.)

There is no need for formal "means testing" because the UBI distribution automatically distributes spending money to those who need it most. For example, if we give $500 per month to everyone, the rich simply bank the whole amount, the middle class spend some and save some, and the poor spend almost all. Since the rich saved theirs, it did not go into general circulation, and more money must be issued to keep us at the top of the production parabola. Every dollar saved by the rich results in a dollar being automatically distributed to the poor and middle class.

Once the legislation is passed, we will need some guidelines for implementing the legislation.

SECTION 5

IMPLEMENTATION GUIDELINES

1. Continue to distribute UBI progress dollars in ever-increasing amounts until demand-pull inflation is observed.

There are several types of inflation. <u>Demand-pull inflation is "too many dollars chasing too few goods."</u> An example of this occurred during the early 1980s when a decade of baby boomers overwhelmed our economy with increased demand for housing and loans to purchase those houses. The price of houses and interest rates shot up fast enough to induce spiraling inflation. <u>Spiraling inflation, also referred to as built-in inflation, is a condition when employees start asking for wage increases to maintain their same standard of living</u>. Spiraling inflation is risky because it can lead to run-away or hyper-inflation, a condition that is to be avoided at all costs.

When I graduated from high school in 1966, nine in ten Americans could buy a house. When I graduated from college in 1971, seven in ten Americans could buy a house. When my wife and I purchased our first house in 1976 (for $30,000), three in ten Americans could buy a house. (I was actually called a fool by an older employee in another section for paying so much. He had bought a 50% larger house a few years earlier for only two-thirds as much. His advice was to wait until prices came back down.) By 1982 only one American in ten could buy a house. In 1982, there were three vacant lots at the end of our block selling for $22,000 apiece. I inquired about purchasing one of them and found out that I could not qualify to buy a lot in the neighborhood where we now owned a house!

Per Google:

> By 1981, inflation had risen to 9.5%. The Federal Reserve combated inflation by increasing the federal funds rate, an overnight benchmark rate that banks charge each other. Continued hikes in the fed funds rate pushed mortgage rates to an all-time high of 18.45% in 1981. Although the Fed's strategy helped push inflation back to normal levels by the end of 1982, mortgage rates remained mostly in the double-digits for the rest of the decade.

The high mortgage rates crushed the housing construction industry and made it almost impossible for most (even two-salary professionals) to buy a house.

During demand-pull inflation, progress dollar UBI payments should be maintained, but not increased.

2. **Allow at least six months between raises, during the early years until we get near the top of the production parabola. After getting to the top of the production parabola, a raise review should be conducted once a year.**

When people first receive the UBI, some will be spent, some will be used to pay off debt, and some will go into savings. We need to be mindful not to overpay when money is not spent in the general economy. Past credit card and school loan debt are likely to soak up a sizeable share of early payments. After most credit card and school loan debt is paid off, a torrent of money could flood the economy putting us into a seller's market demand-pull inflation. *The demand-pull inflation would require UBI progress dollar payment increases to be paused and the Federal Reserve to raise interest rates.*

3. During cost-push inflation, progress dollar payment increases should continue.

Cost-push inflation is price rises caused by non-typical events like the coronavirus pandemic, fuel political issues, climate change, bird flu, war, etc. During these periods, production disruptions ripple through the economy, causing economic pain to our citizens. A small increase in the UBI progress dollar payment will be welcome.

The key to overcoming cost-push inflation is patience, capitalism, and the maintenance of consumer buying power.

The use of interest rate hikes combined with a lack of UBI is financially painful and will cause our citizens to ask for raises speeding up spiraling inflation. Misdiagnosing the root cause of rising prices as demand-pull inflation when we are in cost-push inflation will cause us to take money out of the economy when we should be putting more money into the economy.

So why haven't we adopted UBI Progress Dollars? We got side-tracked by Modern Monetary Theory.

THE PROBLEM WITH MODERN MONETARY THEORY
IT'S NOT MODERN ENOUGH.

From the 1970s to about 2000, a collection of ideas was developed into Modern Monetary theory. The basic idea was that a country with its own currency could never go broke if its debt were issued in its currency. Should a nation need to pay debts, it can print more money.

As long as this debt-relief tool was employed modestly, the expected inflation from increasing the money supply never seemed to be a problem. *One reason the inflation was less than expected is that we had entered the deflationary part of the production parabola.*

We experienced a period of ultra-low interest rates and ever-increasing government spending without any meaningful inflation until the Covid pandemic became a world problem in 2020. The pandemic, bird flu, a tree beetle in Canada, war in Ukraine, and weather problems caused significant cost-push inflation. Raising interest rates made inflation worse. Also, many companies used inflation to mask price increases. These seven factors pushed prices upward to uncomfortable levels. To return to normal levels, we need UBI progress dollars to maintain consumer demand, lower interest rates, and patience to let capitalism work its magic.

The graph of public debt shows the slope rising at a modest pace until 2008 and then rising at a steeper rate after that time. The steeper rise after 2008 suggests the adoption of MMT (Modern Monetary Theory) had become a more pervasive concept in our national financial management.

Public debt of the United States from 1990 to 2022

(in billion U.S. dollars)

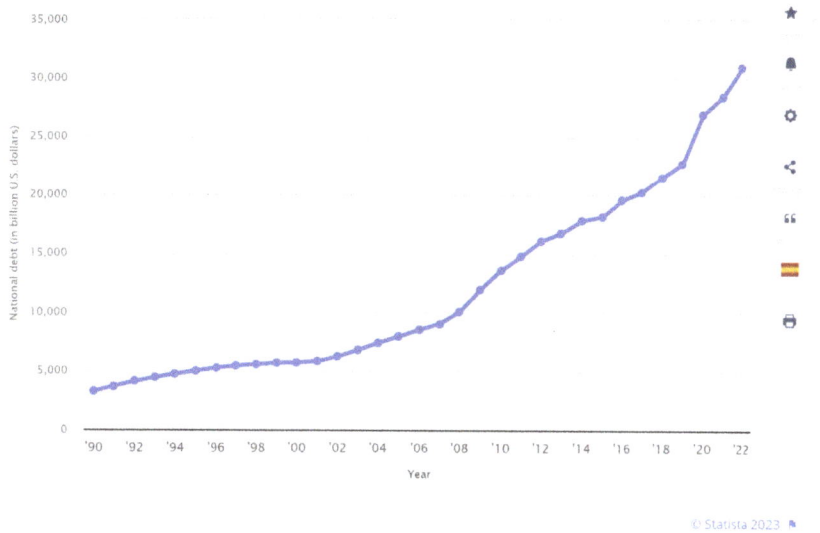

One big fear of increased deficit spending was that it would kickstart inflation. If we had indulged in such high levels of deficit spending before 2000 (a seller's market), we would likely kick off high inflation. However, much to the amazement of many, we got lower inflation.

Annual inflation rate in the United States from 1990 to 2022

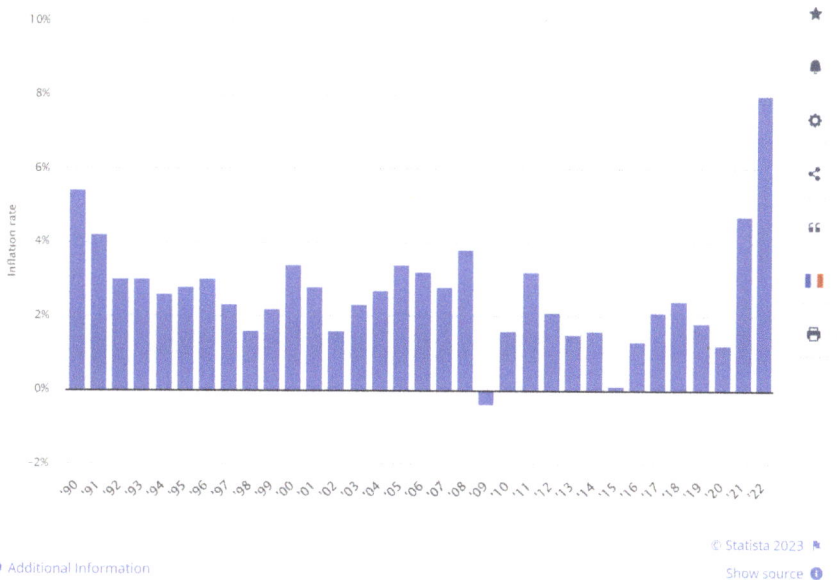

The United States national debt (chart below), adjusted to 2022 dollars, shows a very steep upward slope after 2002. We could "get away" with spending beyond our income without causing inflation. So, we did.

U.S. National Debt Over the Last 100 Years
Inflation Adjusted - 2022 Dollars

2022	$30.93 T
Fiscal Year	Total Debt

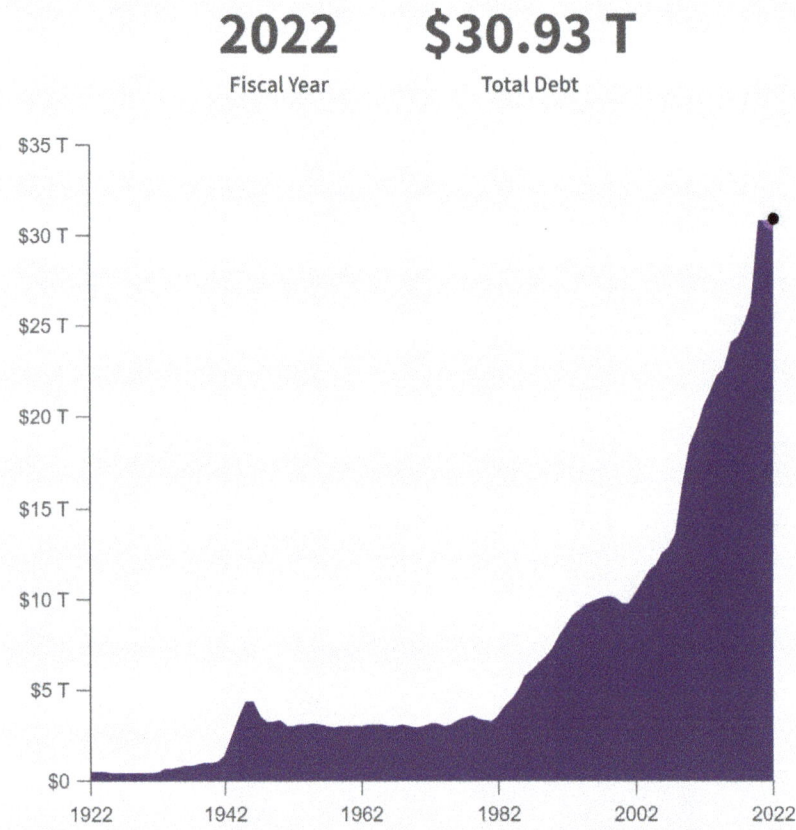

Visit the Historical Debt Outstanding dataset to explore and download this data. The inflation data is sourced from the Bureau of Labor Statistics.

Last Updated: September 30, 2022

The main weakness of MMT is that it does not address our biggest problem, an ever-weaker consumer demand. The money spent seldom went to the poor or dwindling middle class. Government infrastructure projects and defense spending did not "trickle down" to the wage-slave consumers. Most of the money went to the "fat-cat" contractors who owned the machines. After one spending effort, President Obama complained that it took about $270,000 of taxpayer money to generate just one job.

A *second weakness of MMT is that money was borrowed*. Since we were deficit spending beyond the taxpayer dollars we received, we had to borrow money to pay for infrastructure improvements. The interest on that debt is mortgaging our children's future. In 2022, the Congressional Budget Office estimated that the interest payments on the national debt would exceed our federal defense budget in 2029! That doesn't leave much for social programs, education, etc.

LESSONS LEARNED FROM MMT

1. We can send extra money into the economy without causing harmful inflation because we are on the buyer's market (too few dollars chasing too many goods) side of the production parabola.

2. Deficit spending requires accumulating debt that becomes a future interest bill. UBI Progress Dollars are never repaid, so the next generation has no future interest burden.

3. Our central planning projects helped rehabilitate old structures but did not get enough money into the hands of consumers.

4. Once again, "Trickle Down" did not work. Giving large jobs to heavily mechanized firms with few workers did not provide sufficient money to the bottom 90% of us to increase national consumer demand.

5. Modern Monetary Theory does not significantly address weakening consumer demand in the 21st century. Our consumer-corporation economy will worsen as consumer demand drops due to wages lost when machines replace human jobs. UBI Progress Dollars from a non-taxpayer account must be distributed directly to all American adults. The days of giving automation-intensive corporations projects to get sufficient cash into consumers' hands are over. If we need additional stimulus, we must bypass the machines and give money directly to American citizens.

UNIVERSAL BASIC INCOME WE CAN'T GET UBI WITHOUT PROGRESS DOLLARS

The need for Universal Basic Income (UBI) is frequently stated because many people fear that machines are taking so many jobs that increasing numbers of humans will be without enough income to care for themselves. Most UBI proposals are poorly defined schemes that do not specify how the UBI will be funded and do not consider inflation or other consequences.

An example is from a June 5, 2016, BBC newscast reporting a vote in Switzerland on a proposed monthly UBI amount of $2555 for adults and a quarter of that for children. No funding details were specified. Swiss voters rejected the proposal by 77% to 23%.

Some small trials with UBI for select groups in various nations have addressed one big concern: will people stop working once they receive UBI? The answer is no. Most people receiving UBI continued to work.

The lack of UBI success comes from a surprising deficiency—a proper number! The number of dollars per month that UBI advocates request is usually a round number pulled from thin air. Thus far, they have tried to finance UBI from a very unpopular source, increased taxes. The number selected is not related to the economy. Instead, it is loosely associated with an estimate of perceived need. There are no provisions for increasing the amount over time.

If UBI advocates switched to UBI Progress Dollars from the Production Parabola, they might attain instant success.

1. UBI Progress Dollars have a number of dollars per month that is equal to the wages lost to machines. The problem with arbitrary UBI numbers is that we get demand-pull inflation if they are too high. If they are too low, we reduce economic activity. The GDP per person drops. If we continue waiting to implement UBI, the economy will get smaller and smaller, and so will the UBI annuity.

2. UBI Progress dollars are tied to the economy. Every time technology replaces humans, the UBI rises.

3. UBI Progress dollars are not funded by tax increases. UBI Progress dollars are taken from an account that must never be repaid.

4. UBI Progress dollars do not cause inflation. They are raised until a minor amount of demand-pull inflation is observed. At that point, increases in UBI progress dollars are paused.

5. UBI Progress dollars do not require a large bureaucracy to determine who gets how much. Instead, every adult citizen receives the same monthly amount.

6. UBI Progress dollars do not cause individuals to quit working like welfare. With welfare, you lose benefits if you go back to work. UBI Progress dollars have no such disincentive to find employment because you get the same level of UBI progress dollars regardless of how much you earn on your job.

7. UBI Progress dollars provide an instant flow of money once UBI is adopted. This immediately benefits young people by giving them money to help fund their higher education, start a business, or get married. The modest amount of money would greatly help seniors struggling to survive on social security.

I encourage all UBI advocates to champion a Progress Dollar UBI. We need the Start-up Universal Basic Income as soon as possible to assist our citizens and optimize our economic growth.

There is hope.

FINAL OBSERVATIONS

Western industrialized nations have experienced problems similar to the United States since 2000. We have been forced to deficit spend in an effort to replace the consumer demand lost to automation. Now, the interest payments on those debts are getting too big. If we had recognized the production parabola concept and started paying out progress dollars to consumers in 2000, we would have much smaller national debts today.

Major German car maker Volkswagen is closing three plants, giving the reason that its German customers are "getting poorer." Governments are collapsing as they lose the confidence of voters. Elected officials' adherence to outdated seller's market economic ideals has led to lower standards of living, declining birthrates, and anger at our failing institutions (including the people who run them) because there is little or no hope for a better economic future.

We have crossed over the top of the production parabola into the buyer's market (too few dollars chasing too many goods). Increases in production capacity have made our consumers so poor (through unemployment and underemployment) that production must be decreased to avoid excess inventory. We see this every day with the announcement of more store closings.

Our decline is just starting. As the middle classes become increasingly poorer, social instability will increase. Even the rich will lose money as their corporations are forced to shrink to match declining demand for all products. Moving corporations elsewhere is a temporary solution doomed to failure. Poorer nations will become destitute as their formerly rich nation customers become poorer. War and martial law will likely increase.

Our ability to reverse the downward trend decreases with every plant closing, every store closing, and every business failure. Losing more productive capacity is not the answer.

The responsibility for our economic demise rests squarely on the shoulders of our elected officials. They must become elected leaders who recognize the importance of economic demand and institute the progress dollar automation annuity. Our fate is in their hands.

www.ingramcontent.com/pod-product-compliance
Lightning Source LLC
Chambersburg PA
CBHW052345210326
41597CB00037B/6265